THE EXECUTIVE'S
QUOTATION BOOK

THE EXECUTIVE'S QUOTATION BOOK

A Corporate Companion

Edited by James Charlton

St. Martin's Press   *New York*

Design by Laura Hammond

Library of Congress Cataloging in Publication Data
Main entry under title:
    The Executive's quotation book.

    Includes index.
    1. Business—Quotations, maxims, etc. 2. Management—Quotations, maxims, etc. 3. Money—Quotations, maxims, etc. I. Charlton, James, 1939-   .
HF5351.E95   1983   650   83-16067
ISBN 0-312-27431-9

10 9 8 7 6 5 4

FOREWORD

I like quotations. There is something about the short form that appeals to me. Maybe it has to do with our diminished attention spans—"Quotations are the literary form of the '80s," to quote one wag—but I prefer to think that quotations are a distillation of wit and thought imposed by the brevity of the form. Quotations are not only entertaining to read, they can be provocative and useful. Nothing shores up an argument or provides an authoritative cap to some conversation like the proper quote; it reflects our education, our erudition. Many times a quote can substitute for a sentiment or sentence that we ourselves would not dare utter. But put quotation marks around it and attribute it to Twain or Wilde and you can get away unscathed.

"Every quotation contributes something to the stability and enlargement of the language," said Samuel Johnson, and I agree. *Good* quotes—those that make their way into the consciousness of a people—seem almost to spring up on their own. Oftentimes they are attributed to people who never said them, or who said them in quite a different form or context. We take them up and edit, shape and polish them to fit our needs. Whether Leo Durocher ever said, "Nice guys finish last," when referring to the Dodgers, doesn't matter. The phrase was too perfect, too useful in a variety of situations, to let die.

The financial and business worlds are particularly rich fields for quotations, since they are areas that touch all our lives. Opinions, reflections, regrets, gloatings, admonishments, warnings and advice abound. Some are pompous; others are humble and reflect a very non-corporate view of the world. Many of the wittiest come not just from the established humorists such as Mark Twain, Will Rogers and Oscar Wilde, but from unexpected sources such as Robert Frost and J. Paul Getty, both of whom are marvelously funny on the subject of business.

The Executive's Quotation Book is not meant to be all-inclusive, even in the subject areas we've staked out for it. I have been a collector of quotations for years, clipping favorites from newspapers or magazines and stuffing them in folders and drawers. Many of those included here are a result of those efforts. A number of others have been sent along by friends and acquaintances, and to them I owe a debt of gratitude. Then there are a number of larger sources of quotations, wonderful compendiums such as *Bartlett's Familiar Quotations*, *Peter's Quotations*, *The Fitzhenry and Whiteside Book of Quotations*, that I acknowledge, respect and recommend for everyone's library. To those books I leave subject lists, key words, first line indexes and such. At the request of Barbara Anderson and Nina Barrett, two patient and supportive editors who shared my enjoyment of the subject, there is an index of names. While the quotations are arranged loosely according to subject matter, they need not be read in any particular order. Whether you start at the beginning or dip in at the middle doesn't matter—as long as you enjoy the book.

THE EXECUTIVE'S
QUOTATION BOOK

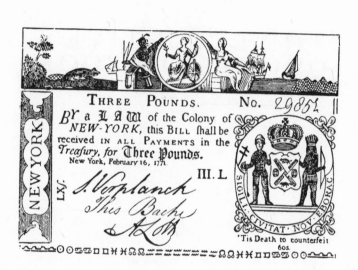

THREE POUNDS.   No. 29852

BY a *LAW* of the Colony of
NEW-YORK, this BILL shall be
received IN ALL PAYMENTS in the
Treasury, for **Three Pounds.**
New York, February 16, 1771.

NEW YORK

LX/.   III. L

S. Vooplanch
This Bache
Ad Lott

SIGILL. CIVITAT. NOV. EBORAC

'Tis Death to counterfeit
60s.

Money is the wise man's religion.
EURIPIDES

Money, which represents the prose of life, and is hardly spoken of in parlors without apology, is, in its effects and laws, as beautiful as roses.
RALPH WALDO EMERSON

You can be as romantic as you please about love, Hector; but you musn't be romantic about money.
GEORGE BERNARD SHAW

Money, it turned out, was exactly like sex; you thought of nothing else if you didn't have it and thought of other things if you did.
JAMES BALDWIN

Money is like manure. You have to spread it around or it smells.
J. PAUL GETTY

Money is the poor people's credit card.
MARSHALL MCLUHAN

I've been in trouble all my life; I've done the most unutterable rubbish, all because of money. I didn't need it. . . the lure of the zeros was simply too great.
RICHARD BURTON

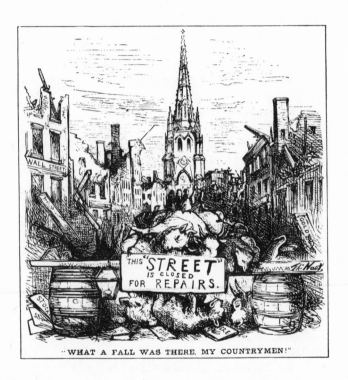

".. WHAT A FALL WAS THERE, MY COUNTRYMEN!"

If women didn't exist, all the money in the world would have no meaning.

ARISTOTLE ONASSIS

Make money and the whole world will conspire to call you a gentleman.

MARK TWAIN

The greater the wealth, the thicker will be the dirt. This undoubtedly describes a tendency of our time.

JOHN KENNETH GALBRAITH

So you think that money is the root of all evil. Have you ever asked what is the root of money?

AYN RAND

Not to be covetous is money in your purse; not to be eager to buy is income.

CICERO

The covetous man never has money; the prodigal will have none shortly.

BEN JONSON

I would rather have my people laugh at my economics than weep for my extravagance.

OSCAR II OF SWEDEN

Who needs money when you're funny.
RANDY NEWMAN

The petty economics of the rich are just as amazing as the silly extravagances of the poor.
WILLIAM FEATHER

Money is a terrible master, but an excellent servant.
P.T. BARNUM

The use of money is all the advantage there is in having money.
BENJAMIN FRANKLIN

The value of money is that with it we can tell any man to go to the devil. It is the sixth sense, which enables you to enjoy the other five.
W. SOMERSET MAUGHAM

Money may be the husk of many things, but not the kernel. It brings you food, but not appetite; medicine, but not health; acquaintances, but not friends; servants, but not faithfulness; days of joy, but not peace or happiness.
HENRIK IBSEN

I believe in the dollar. Everything I earn, I spend!
JOAN CRAWFORD

There are three great friends: an old wife, an old dog, and ready money.

BENJAMIN FRANKLIN

Money and time are the heaviest burdens of life, and the unhappiest of all mortals are those who have more of either than they know what to do.

SAMUEL JOHNSON

Too much of a good thing can be wonderful.

MAE WEST

Everything in the world may be endured except continued prosperity.

GOETHE

The entire essence of America is the hope to first make money—then make money with money—then make lots of money with lots of money.

PAUL ERDMAN

The highest use of capital is not to make money, but to make money do more for the betterment of life.

HENRY FORD

The more money an American accumulates, the less interesting he becomes.

GORE VIDAL

A feast is made for laughter,
And wine maketh merry,
But money answereth all things.
ECCLESIASTES 10:19

The man who damns money has obtained it dishonor-
ably; the man who respects it has earned it.
AYN RAND

When a fellow says, "It ain't the money but the principle
of the thing," it's the money.
FRANK MCKINNEY "KIN" HUBBARD

Finance is the art of passing currency from hand to hand
until it finally disappears.
ROBERT SARNOFF

Finance is the art or science of managing revenues and
resources for the best advantage of the manager.
AMBROSE BIERCE

Where large sums of money are concerned, it is advisable
to trust nobody.
AGATHA CHRISTIE

Those heroes of finance are like beads on a string—when
one slips off, the rest follow.
HENRIK IBSEN

I don't want to make money. I just want to be wonderful.
MARILYN MONROE

I don't want to be a star, I want to be a millionaire.
"KINKY" FRIEDMAN

Surplus wealth is a sacred trust which its possessor is bound to administer in his lifetime for the good of the community.
ANDREW CARNEGIE

Prosperity is only an instrument to be used, not a deity to be worshipped.
CALVIN COOLIDGE

Make money your God, and it will plague you like the devil.
HENRY FIELDING

There is nothing wrong with men possessing riches but the wrong comes when riches possess men.
BILLY GRAHAM

You know, Ernest, the rich are different from us.
F. SCOTT FITZGERALD

Yes, I know. They have more money.
ERNEST HEMINGWAY

Paying attention to simple little things that most men neglect makes a few men rich.

HENRY FORD

As a general rule, nobody has money who ought to have it.

BENJAMIN DISRAELI

Sudden money is going from zero to two hundred dollars a week. The rest doesn't count.

NEIL SIMON

The only way to keep score in business is to add up how much money you make.

HARRY HELMSLEY

If you can count your money, you don't have a billion dollars.

J. PAUL GETTY

The end is easily foretold,
When every blessed thing you hold
Is made of silver, or of gold,
You long for simple pewter.
When you have nothing else to wear
But long for cloth of gold and satins rare,
For cloth of gold you cease to care
Up goes the price of shoddy.

W.S. GILBERT *(Gilbert & Sullivan)*

I've been rich and I've been poor, and believe me, rich is better

JOE E. LEWIS

I've never been poor, only broke. Being poor is a frame of mind. Being broke is only a temporary situation.

MIKE TODD

I have tried to become conservative. In 1958 I resolved to be simply a piano player. That was the year I lost $800,000.

LIBERACE

That money talks
I'll not deny,
I heard it once:
It said, "Goodbye"

RICHARD ARMOUR

Neither great poverty nor great riches will hear reason.

HENRY FIELDING

Poor people know poor people and rich people know rich people. It is one of the few things La Rochefoucauld did not say, but then La Rouchefoucauld never lived in the Bronx.

MOSS HART

The chief problem of the lower-income farmers is poverty.

NELSON ROCKEFELLER

There is a serious tendency towards capitalism among the well-to-do peasants.

MAO TSE TUNG

The trouble with being poor is that it takes up all your time.

WILLIAM DE KOONING

Poverty is uncomfortable; but nine times out of ten the best thing that can happen to a young man is to be tossed overboard and compelled to sink or swim.

JAMES A. GARFIELD

Almost all the noblest things that have been achieved in the world have been achieved by poor men, poor scholars, poor professional men, poets, and men of genius. A certain staidness and sobriety, a certain moderation and restraint, a certain pressure of circumstances are good for men. His body was not made for luxuries. It sickens, sinks and dies under them.

HENRY DAVID THOREAU

I'd like to live like a poor man with lots of money.

PABLO PICASSO

I never wanted to be a millionaire. I just wanted to live like one.

WALTER HAGEN

Mamma may have
Papa may have
But God bless the child that's got his own.
That's got his own.

BILLIE HOLIDAY

Money is always there but the pockets change; it is not in the same pockets after a change, and that is all there is to say about money.

GERTRUDE STEIN

Most people seek after what they do not possess and are enslaved by the very things they want to acquire.

ANWAR EL-SADAT

Property is the fruit of labor; property is desirable; it is a positive good in the world. That some should be rich shows that others may become rich, and, hence, is just another encouragement to industry and enterprise.

ABRAHAM LINCOLN

Government has no other end but the preservation of property.

JOHN LOCKE

It is preoccupation with possession, more than anything else, that prevents men from living freely and nobly.
BERTRAND RUSSELL

Possessions, outward success, publicity, luxury—to me these have always been contemptible. I believe that a simple and unassuming manner of life is best for everyone, best both for the body and the mind.
ALBERT EINSTEIN

In God we trust, all others pay cash.
Sign used in retail stores during the Depression

Neither a borrower nor a lender be;
For loan oft loses both itself and friend,
And borrowing dulls the edge of husbandry.
WILLIAM SHAKESPEARE

It is better to give than to lend, and it costs about the same.
SIR PHILIP GIBBS

Let us all be happy and live within our means, even if we have to borrow the money to do it with.
C.F. BROWNE (ARTEMUS WARD)

I get by with a little help from my friends.
JOHN LENNON & PAUL MCCARTNEY

Credit buying is much like being drunk. The buzz happens immediately and gives you a lift. . . . The hangover comes the day after.

DR. JOYCE BROTHERS

Economy is in itself a source of great revenue.

SENECA

The human species, according to the best theory and form of it, is composed of two distinct races, *the men who borrow, and the men who lend*.

CHARLES LAMB

Do you know the only thing that gives me pleasure? It's seeing my dividends roll in.

JOHN D. ROCKEFELLER, JR.

Never invest your money in anything that eats or needs repairing.

BILLY ROSE

There is nothing so disastrous as a rational investment policy in an irrational world.

JOHN MAYNARD KEYNES

There are only two times in a man's life when he should not speculate; when he can't afford it, and when he can.

MARK TWAIN

There is scarcely an instance of a man who has made a fortune by speculation and kept it.

ANDREW CARNEGIE

There is no moral difference between gambling at cards or in lotteries or on the race track and gambling in the stock market. One method is just as pernicious to the body politic as the other kind, and in degree the evil worked is far greater.

THEODORE ROOSEVELT

One of these days in your travels a guy is going to come up to you and show you a nice brand-new deck of cards on which the seal is not yet broken, and this guy is going to offer to bet you that he can make the jack of spades jump out of the deck and squirt cider in your ear. But, son, do not bet this man, for as sure as you stand there, you are going to wind up with an earful of cider.

DAMON RUNYON

The bulls make money
The bears make money
But the pigs get slaughtered.
Wall Street axiom

With an evening coat and a white tie, even a stockbroker can gain a reputation for being civilized.

OSCAR WILDE

Wall Street. A thoroughfare that begins in a graveyard and ends in a river.

ANONYMOUS

October is one of the peculiarly dangerous months to speculate in stocks. The others are July, January, September, April, November, May, March, June, December, August and February.

MARK TWAIN

There is no more mean, stupid, pitiful, selfish, ungrateful animal than the stock-speculating public. It is the greatest of cowards, for it is afraid of itself.

WILLIAM HAZLITT

It is a socialist idea that making profits is a vice; I consider the real vice is making losses.

WINSTON CHURCHILL

There is much more hope for humanity from manufacturers who enjoy their work than from those who continue in the irksome business of founding hospitals.

ALFRED NORTH WHITEHEAD

The worst crime against working people is a company which fails to operate at a profit.

SAMUEL L. GOMPERS

There are poor men in this country who cannot be bought: the day I found that out, I sent my gold abroad.
COMTESSE DE VOIGRAND

Buy land, they're not making it anymore.
MARK TWAIN

Invest in inflation. It is the only thing going up.
WILL ROGERS

Inflation is the one form of taxation that can be imposed without legislation.
MILTON FRIEDMAN

We have a love-hate relationship. We hate inflation, but we love everything that causes it.
WILLIAM SIMON

Inflation can be conquered by the continued application of public and private restraint, and by attention to long-run political policies that increase supply and productivity.
CHARLES SCHULTZE

If people believe that there will be a marked decrease in the rate of inflation, that might be a self-fulfilling set of beliefs.
WILLIAM BAUMOL, *president of the American Economics Association*

A nickel ain't worth a dime anymore.
YOGI BERRA

The way to stop financial joy-riding is to arrest the chauffeur, not the automobile.
WOODROW WILSON

What's money? A man is a success if he gets up in the morning and gets to bed at night, and in between he does what he wants to.
BOB DYLAN

All you need in this life is ignorance and confidence, and then success is sure.
MARK TWAIN

It is no wisdom ever to commend or discommend the actions of men by their success; for oftentimes some enterprises attempted by good counsel end unfortunately, and others inadvisedly taken in hand have happy success.
SIR WALTER RALEIGH

The best thing that can come with success is the knowledge that it is nothing to long for.
LIV ULLMANN

Success has always been a great liar.
FRIEDRICH NIETZSCHE

The success of each is dependent upon the success of the other.

JOHN D. ROCKEFELLER, JR.

Nothing succeeds like success.

ENGLISH PROVERB

It is not enough to succeed. Others must fail.

GORE VIDAL

The moral flabbiness born of the bitch-goddess SUC-CESS. That—with the squalid interpretation put on the word success—is our national disease.

WILLIAM JAMES

The most successful businessman is the man who holds onto the old just as long as it good, and grabs the new just as soon as it is better.

ROBERT P. VANDERPOEL

The successful people are the ones who can think up stuff for the rest of the world to keep busy at.

DON MARQUIS

The toughest thing about success is that you've got to keep on being a success. Talent is only a starting point in business. You've got to keep working that talent.

IRVING BERLIN

Every successful enterprise requires three men—a dreamer, a businessman, and a son-of-a-bitch.
PETER MCARTHUR

The secret of Japanese success is not technology, but a special way of managing people—a style that focuses a strong company philosophy, a distinct corporate culture, long-range staff development, and consensus decision-making.
WILLIAM OUCHI

No man lives without jostling and being jostled; in all ways he has to elbow himself through the world, giving and receiving offense.
PLAUTUS

Each citizen contributes to the revenues of the State a portion of his property in order that his tenure of the rest may be secure.
MONTESQUIEU

The power to tax . . . is not only the power to destroy but also the power to keep alive.
UNITED STATES SUPREME COURT

The nation should have a tax system that looks like someone designed it on purpose.
WILLIAM SIMON

When there is an income tax, the just man will pay more and the unjust less on the same amount of income.
PLATO

Taxes are what we pay for a civilized society.
OLIVER WENDELL HOLMES, JR.

There is nothing sinister in so arranging one's affairs as to keep taxes as low as possible.
JUDGE LEARNED HAND

The hardest thing in the world to understand is the income tax.
ALBERT EINSTEIN

The income tax has made more liars out of the American people than golf has. Even when you make a tax form out on the level, you don't know, when it's through, if you are a crook or a martyr.
WILL ROGERS

The entire graduated income tax structue was created by Karl Marx.
RONALD REAGAN

From each according to his abilities, to each according to his needs.
KARL MARX

I have no use for bodyguards, but I have very special use for two highly trained certified public accountants.
ELVIS PRESLEY

There have been three great inventions since the beginning of time: fire, the wheel, and central banking.
WILL ROGERS

Banking establishments are more dangerous than standing armies.
THOMAS JEFFERSON

Banking may well be a career from which no man really recovers.
JOHN KENNETH GALBRAITH

A sound banker, Alas! is not one who foresees danger and avoids it, but one who, when he is ruined, is ruined in a conventional and orthodox way along with his fellows so that no one can really blame him.
JOHN MAYNARD KEYNES

A banker is a fellow who lends you his umbrella when the sun is shining and wants it back the minute it begins to rain.
MARK TWAIN

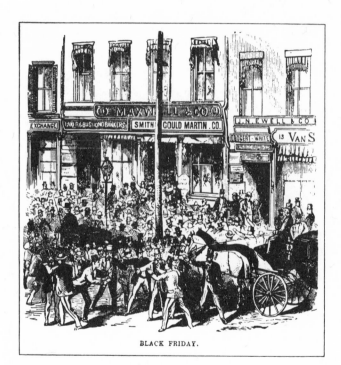

BLACK FRIDAY.

One rule which woe betides the banker who fails to heed it . . . Never lend any money to anybody unless they don't need it.

OGDEN NASH

It is rather a pleasant experience to be alone in a bank at night.

WILLIE SUTTON

If you owe a bank enough money you own it.

ANONYMOUS

The banks couldn't afford me. That's why I had to be in business for myself.

SAMUEL GOLDWYN

It's so American to start one's own business.

ANNE MCDONNELL FORD

I'm self-employed.

PRINCE PHILLIP

In soloing—as in other activities—it is far easier to start something than it is to finish it.

AMELIA EARHART

Consultant: any ordinary guy more than fifty miles from home.

ERIC SEVAREID

The real problem is what to do with the problem solvers after the problems are solved.

GAY TALESE

Management consultants are people who borrow your watch to tell you what time it is, and then walk off with it.

ROBERT TOWNSEND

The ability to deal with people is as purchasable a commodity as sugar or coffee. And I pay more for that ability than for any other under the sun.

JOHN D. ROCKEFELLER, JR.

The greatest ability in business is to get along with others and influence their actions. A chip on the shoulder is too heavy a piece of baggage to carry through life.

JOHN HANCOCK

When two men in business always agree, one of them is unnecessary.

WILLIAM WRIGLEY, JR.

It were not best that we should all think alike; it is difference of opinion that makes horse races.

MARK TWAIN

Every kind of peaceful cooperation among men is primarily based on mutual trust and only secondarily on institutions such as courts of justice and police.

ALBERT EINSTEIN

Nice guys finish last.

LEO DUROCHER

An eminent lawyer cannot be a dishonest man. Tell me a man is dishonest and I will answer he is no lawyer. He cannot be, because he is careless and reckless of justice; the law is not in his heart, is not the standard and rule of his conduct.

DANIEL WEBSTER

I don't want a lawyer to tell me what I cannot do; I hire him to tell me how to do what I want to do.

J. P. MORGAN

The first thing we do, let's kill all the lawyers.

WILLIAM SHAKESPEARE

What's the first excellence in a lawyer? Tautology. What the second? Tautology. What the third? Tautology.

RICHARD STEELE

Necessity has no law; I know some attorneys of the same.

BENJAMIN FRANKLIN

I think we may class the lawyer in the natural history of monsters.

JOHN KEATS

An oral contract isn't worth the paper it's written on.

SAMUEL GOLDWYN

He is no lawyer who cannot take two sides.

CHARLES LAMB

It is the trade of lawyers to question everything, yield nothing, and to talk by the hour.

THOMAS JEFFERSON

Lawyers have been known to wrest from reluctant juries triumphant verdicts of acquittal for their clients, even when those clients, as often happens, were clearly and unmistakably innocent.

OSCAR WILDE

Lawyers make a living trying to figure out what other lawyers have written.

WILL ROGERS

Whether you're an honest man or whether you're a thief depends on whose solicitor has given me a brief.

W. S. GILBERT *(Gilbert & Sullivan)*

Discourage litigation. Persuade your neighbor to compromise whenever you can. As a peacemaker the lawyer has a superior opportunity of being a good man. There will still be business enough.

ABRAHAM LINCOLN

Work is love made visible.

KAHLIL GIBRAN

The labourer is worthy of his hire.

NEW TESTAMENT

Business underlies eveything in our national life, including our spiritual life. Witness the fact that in the Lord's prayer, the first petition is for daily bread. No one can worship God or love his neighbor on an empty stomach.

WOODROW WILSON

Man matures through work which inspires him to difficult good.

POPE JOHN PAUL II

Don't tell me how hard you work. Tell me how much you get done.

JAMES LING

When your work speaks for itself, don't interrupt.

HENRY KAISER

34

As others toil for me, I must toil for others.
ECCLESIASTES 2:20

If he works for you, you work for him.
JAPANESE PROVERB

The man who is employed for wages is as much a businessman as his employer.
WILLIAM JENNINGS BRYAN

It is not the employer who pays wages—he only handles the money. It is the product that pays wages.
HENRY FORD

There are two things needed in these days; first, for rich men to find out how poor men live; and, second, for poor men to know how rich men work.
E. ATKINSON

People of privilege will always risk their complete destruction rather than surrender any material part of their advantage.
JOHN KENNETH GALBRAITH

It is easier to do a job right than to explain why you didn't.
MARTIN VAN BUREN

36

Work is of two kinds: first, altering the position of matter at or near the earth's surface relatively to the other matter; second, telling other people to do so. The first kind is unpleasant and ill paid; the second is pleasant and highly paid.

BERTRAND RUSSELL

In a hierarchy, every employee tends to rise to his level of incompetence.

LAURENCE PETER

If A equals success, then the formula is A equals X plus Y, with X being work, Y play, and Z keeping your mouth shut.

ALBERT EINSTEIN

The world is full of willing people; some willing to work, the rest willing to let them.

ROBERT FROST

It never fails: everybody who really makes it does it by busting his ass.

ALAN ARKIN

I worked for charity all my life and now it's kind of fun to work for money.

CHARLOTTE FORD

I've always worried about people who are willing to work for nothing. Sometimes that's all you get from them, nothing.

SAM ERVIN

Those who work much do not work hard.

HENRY DAVID THOREAU

I never knew a man escape failures, in either mind or body, who worked seven days in a week.

SIR ROBERT PEEL

My rule always was to do the business of the day in the day.

DUKE OF WELLINGTON

There is more to life than increasing its speed.

MAHATMA GANDHI

Opportunities are usually disguised as hard work, so most people don't recognize them.

ANN LANDERS

Small opportunities are often the beginning of great enterprise.

DEMOSTHENES

Luck means the hardships and privations which you have not hesitated to endure, the long nights you have devoted to work. Luck means the appointments you have never failed to keep; the trains you have never failed to catch.

MAX O'RELL

Progress in industry depends very largely on the enterprise of deep-thinking men who are ahead of the times in their ideas.

SIR WILLIAM ELLIS

There is hardly anything in the world that some men can't make a little worse and sell a little cheaper, and the people who consider price only are this man's lawful prey.

JOHN RUSKIN

The man who will use his skill and constructive imagination to see how much he can give for a dollar, instead of how little he can give for a dollar, is bound to succeed.

HENRY FORD

I should never have made my success in life if I had not bestowed upon the least thing I have ever undertaken the same attention and care that I have bestowed upon the greatest.

CHARLES DICKENS

If you want to succeed you should strike out on new paths rather than travel the worn paths of accepted success.

JOHN D. ROCKEFELLER, JR.

Technological progress has merely provided us with more efficient means for going backwards.

ALDOUS HUXLEY

You can't sit on the lid of progress. If you do, you will be blown to pieces.

HENRY KAISER

Punctuality is the soul of business.

THOMAS HALIBURTON

Patience is a most necessary quality for business: many a man would rather you heard his story than granted his request.

EARL OF CHESTERFIELD

The better work men do is always done under stress and at great personal cost.

WILLIAM CARLOS WILLIAMS

The reason why worry kills more people than work is that more people worry than work.

ROBERT FROST

Few enterprises of great labor or hard work would be undertaken if we had not the power of magnifying the advantages we expect from them.

SAMUEL JOHNSON

If you aren't fired with enthusiasm, you'll be fired with enthusiasm.

VINCE LOMBARDI

I am a friend of the working man, and I would rather be a friend than be one.

CLARENCE DARROW

Don't be misled into believing that somehow the world owes you a living. The boy who believes that his parents, or the government, or anyone else owes him his livelihood and that he can collect it without labor will wake up one day and find himself working for another boy who did not have that belief and, therefore, earned the right to have others work for him.

DAVID SARNOFF

Like every man of sense and good feeling, I abominate work.

ALDOUS HUXLEY

I do not like work even when another person does it.

MARK TWAIN

My own business bores me to death. I prefer other people's.

OSCAR WILDE

Idleness is only the refuge of weak minds.

EARL OF CHESTERFIELD

The brain is a wonderful organ; it starts working the moment you get up in the morning and doesn't stop until you get into the office.

ROBERT FROST

Anyone can do any amount of work, provided it isn't the work he is *supposed* to be doing at that moment.

ROBERT BENCHLEY

I find that two days' neglect of business to give more discontent in mind than ten times the pleasure thereof can repair again, be it what will.

SAMUEL PEPYS

One must work, if not from inclination, at least out of despair—since it proves on closest examination that work is less boring than amusing oneself.

CHARLES BAUDELAIRE

Work is the curse of the drinking classes.

OSCAR WILDE

Employment, sir, and hardships, prevent melancholy.
SAMUEL JOHNSON

Wanting to work is so rare a want that it should be encouraged.
ABRAHAM LINCOLN

Men can do jointly what they cannot do singly; and the union of minds and hands, the concentration of their power, becomes almost omnipotent.
DANIEL WEBSTER

The workingmen are the basis of all government, for the plain reason that they are the most numerous.
ABRAHAM LINCOLN

When large numbers of men are unable to find work, unemployment results.
CALVIN COOLIDGE

It's a recession when your neighbor loses his job; it's a depression when you lose yours.
HARRY TRUMAN

The long range solution to high unemployment is to increase the incentive for ordinary people to save, invest, work and employ others. We make it costly for employers to employ people, and we subsidize people not to go to work. We have a system that increasingly taxes work and subsidizes nonwork.

MILTON FRIEDMAN

The taxpayer—that's someone who works for the federal government but doesn't have to take a civil service exam.

RONALD REAGAN

You will find men who want to be carried on the shoulders of others, who think that the world owes them a living. They don't seem to see that we must all lift together and pull together.

HENRY FORD

Men always try to keep women out of business so they won't find out how much fun it really is.

VIVIEN KELLEMS

Being a woman is a terribly difficult task, since it consists principally in dealing with men.

JOSEPH CONRAD

The man flaps about with a bunch of feathers; the woman goes to work softly with a cloth.

OLIVER WENDELL HOLMES

47

All women are ambitious naturally.
CHRISTOPHER MARLOWE *and* GEORGE CHAPMAN

All ambitions are lawful except those which climb upward on the miseries or credulities of mankind.
JOSEPH CONRAD

Just as war is too important to be left to the generals, so is an economic crisis too important to be left to the economists or "practical men."
JOHN KENNETH GALBRAITH

Business is a combination of war and sport.
ANDRÉ MAUROIS

The business of America is business.
CALVIN COOLIDGE

Agriculture, manufactures, commerce and navigation, the four pillars of our prosperity, are most thriving when left most to free enterprise.
THOMAS JEFFERSON

The business of government is to keep the government out of business—that is, unless business needs government aid.
WILL ROGERS

As soon as government management begins it upsets the natural equilibrium of industrial relations, and each interference only requires further bureaucratic control until the end is the tyranny of the totalitarian state.

ADAM SMITH *of Glasgow (1776)*

In all that the people can individually do well for themselves, government ought not to interfere.

ABRAHAM LINCOLN

The best minds are not in government. If any were, business would hire them away.

RONALD REAGAN

In business, the competition will bite you if you keep running; if you stand still, they will swallow you.

WILLIAM KNUDSEN

The business system is blessed with a built-in corrective, namely, that one executive's mistakes become his competitor's assets.

LEO CHERNE

Forget your opponents; always play against par.

SAM SNEAD

The trouble in American life today, in business as well as sports, is that too many people are afraid of competition. The result is that, in some circles, people have come to sneer at success, if it costs hard work and training and sacrifice.

KNUTE ROCKNE

Who gives up when behind is cowardly. Who gives up when ahead is foolish.

DR. WILLIAM ARTHUR WARDE

If the spirit of business adventure is killed, this country will cease to hold the foremost position in the world.

ANDREW MELLON

Blessed are the young, for they shall inherit the national debt.

HERBERT HOOVER

The only good budget is a balanced budget.

ADAM SMITH *of Glasgow (1776)*

The only good rule is that the budget should never be balanced—except for an instant when surplus to curb inflation is being altered to a deficit to fight deflation.

WARREN SMITH *of Ann Arbor (1965)*

No nation was ever ruined by trade.
BENJAMIN FRANKLIN

No nation was ever ruined on account of its debts.
ADOLF HITLER

Any government, like any family, can for a year spend a little more than it earns. But you and I know that a continuance of that habit means the poorhouse.
FRANKLIN DELANO ROOSEVELT

There is no art which one government sooner learns of another than that of draining money from the pockets of the people.
ADAM SMITH *of Glasgow (1776)*

The Congress declares that it is the continuing responsibility of the federal government to . . . promote maximum employment, production and purchasing power.
EMPLOYMENT ACT OF 1946

There is no doubt that the real destroyer of the liberties of any people is he who spreads among them bounties, donations, and largess.
PLUTARCH

We work not only to produce but to give value to time.
EUGENE DELACROIX

I have succeeded in getting my actual work down to thirty minutes a day. That leaves me eighteen hours for engineering.

CHARLES STEINMETZ

What we call "creative work" ought not to be called work at all, because it isn't. . . . I imagine that Thomas Edison never did a day's work in his last fifty years.

STEPHEN LEACOCK

Everything comes to him who hustles while he waits.

THOMAS ALVA EDISON

The average person puts only 25% of his energy and ability into his work. The world takes off its hat to those who put in more than 50% of their capacity, and stands on its head for those few and far between souls who devote 100%.

ANDREW CARNEGIE

Work expands so as to fill the time available for its completion.

C. NORTHCOTE PARKINSON

In the ordinary business of life, industry can do anything which genius can do, and very many things which it cannot.

HENRY WARD BEECHER

54

Life is work, and everything you do is so much more experience.

HENRY FORD

Don't bother about genius. Don't worry about being clever. Trust to hard work, perseverence and determination. And the best motto for the long march is: "Don't grumble. Plug on!"

SIR FREDERICK TREVES

Most of life is routine—dull and grubby, but routine is the momentum that keeps a man going. If you wait for inspiration you'll be standing on the corner after the parade is a mile down the street.

BEN NICHOLAS

Concentration is my motto—first honesty, then industry, then concentration.

ANDREW CARNEGIE

The workingmen have been exploited all the way up and down the line by employers, landlords, everybody.

HENRY FORD

What is work? A way to make a living? A way to keep busy? A glue to hold life together? Work is all these things and more. As an activity and as a symbol, work has always preoccupied us. We do it and we think about it. I go on working for the same reason that a hen goes on laying eggs.

H. L. MENCKEN

Perhaps it is this spector that most haunts working men and women: the planned obsolescence of people that is of a piece with the planned obsolescence of the things they make.

STUDS TERKEL

Until you understand Capitalism you do not understand human society as it exists at present.

GEORGE BERNARD SHAW

In these days a great capitalist has deeper roots than a sovereign prince, unless he is very legitimate.

BENJAMIN DISRAELI

I think that Capitalism, wisely managed, can probably be made more efficient for attaining economic ends than any alternate system yet in sight, but that in itself is in many ways extremely objectionable.

JOHN MAYNARD KEYNES

The craft of the merchant is this, bringing a thing from where it abounds to where it is costly.

RALPH WALDO EMERSON

It is well-known what a middleman is: he is a man who bamboozles one party and plunders the other.

BENJAMIN DISRAELI

The by-product is sometimes more valuable than the product.

HAVELOCK ELLIS

Make three correct guesses consecutively and you will establish a reputation as an expert.

LAURENCE PETER

The successful businessman sometimes makes his money by ability and experience, but he generally makes it by mistake.

G. K. CHESTERTON

Be awful nice to 'em going up, because you're going to meet 'em comin' down.

JIMMY DURANTE

Hitch your wagon to a star.

RALPH WALDO EMERSON

The best executive is the one who has sense enough to pick good men to do what he wants done, and self-restraint enough to keep from meddling with them while they do it.

THEODORE ROOSEVELT

A man is to go about his business as if he had not a friend in the world to help him in it.

LORD HALIFAX

A friendship founded on business is better than a business founded on friendship.

JOHN D. ROCKEFELLER, JR.

Business is business.

GEORGE COLEMAN THE YOUNGER

Business is the oldest of the arts, the newest of professions.

LAURENCE LOWELL, *first president of the Harvard Business School*

Avarice, the spur of Industry.

DAVID HUME

Nothing is quite honest that is not commercial, but not everything commercial is honest.

ROBERT FROST

Men of business must not break their word twice.
THOMAS FULLER

Nothing is illegal if a hundred businessmen decide to do it, and that's true anywhere in the world.
ANDREW YOUNG

It is no secret that organized crime in America takes in over forty billion dollars a year. This is quite a profitable sum, especially when one considers that the Mafia spends very little for office supplies.
WOODY ALLEN

Whatever may be the case in the court of morals, there is no legal obligation on the vendor to inform the purchaser that his is under a mistake, not induced by the act of the vendor.
JUSTICE BLACKBURN

What recommends commerce to me is its enterprise and bravery. It does not clasp its hands and pray to Jupiter.
HENRY DAVID THOREAU

There are no new forms of financial fraud; in the last hundred years there have only been small variations of a few classic designs.
JOHN KENNETH GALBRAITH

The first man gets the oyster, the second man gets the shell.

ANDREW CARNEGIE

Eats first, morals after.

BERTOLT BRECHT

The secret in business is to know something that nobody else knows.

ARISTOTLE ONASSIS

Few people do business well who do nothing else.

EARL OF CHESTERFIELD

Too many executives tend to follow the road proved safe, rather than the dynamic approach of self-reliance, individualism and initiative.

LOUIS E. WOLFSON

Business has only two basic functions—marketing and innovation.

PETER DRUCKER

A man is known by the company he organizes.

AMBROSE BIERCE

If ignorance paid dividends, most Americans could make a fortune out of what they don't know about economics.

LUTHER HODGES

The age of Chivalry is gone; that of sophistry, economists, and calculators has succeeded.

EDMUND BURKE

A businessman is a hybrid of a dancer and a calculator.

PAUL VALÉRY

A computer does not substitute for judgement any more
than a pencil substitutes for literacy. But writing without
a pencil is no particular advantage.

ROBERT MCNAMARA

Economists are the great imperialists of the social sci-
ences.

GARDNER ACKLEY

What we might call, by way of eminence, the dismal
science.

THOMAS CARLYLE, *on economics*

An economist is a man who states the obvious in terms of
the incomprehensible.

ALFRED A. KNOPF

Booms and slumps are simply the expression of the
results of an oscillation of the terms of credit about their
equilibrium positions.

JOHN MAYNARD KEYNES

John Stuart Mill,
By a mighty effort of will,
Overcame his natural bonhomie
And wrote *Principals of Political Economy*.
EDMUND CLERIHEW BENTLEY

If all the economists were laid end to end, they'd never reach a conclusion.
GEORGE BERNARD SHAW

The instability of the economy is equaled only by the instability of the economists.
JOHN H. WILLIAMS

I am now a Keynesian.
RICHARD NIXON

We are all Keynesians now.
MILTON FRIEDMAN

In the long run, we are all dead.
JOHN MAYNARD KEYNES

Whenever there are great strains or changes in the economic system, it tends to generate crackpot theories which then find their way into the legislative channels.
DAVID STOCKMAN

Very dangerous things, theories.
DOROTHY SAYERS

Advertising is a valuable economic factor because it is the cheapest way of selling goods, especially if the goods are worthless.
SINCLAIR LEWIS

Advertisements contain the only truths to be relied on in a newspaper.
THOMAS JEFFERSON

Anything you do to enhance sales is a promotion.
BILL VEECK

Promise, large promise, is the soul of an advertisement.
SAMUEL JOHNSON

Advertising is the modern substitute for argument; its function is to make the worse appear better.
GEORGE SANTAYANA

You can tell the ideals of a nation by its advertisements.
NORMAN DOUGLAS

You can fool all of the people all of the time if the advertising is right and the budget is big enough.
JOSEPH E. LEVINE

Advertising is 85% confusion and 15% commission.
FRED ALLEN

The guy you've really got to reach with your advertising is the copywriter for your chief rival's advertising agency. If you can terrorize him, you've got it licked.
HOWARD L. GOSSAGE

The codfish lays 10,000 eggs,
The homely hen just one;
The codfish never cackles
To tell you that she's done.
And so we scorn the codfish,
And the homely hen we prize.
Which demonstrates to you and me
That it pays to advertise.
The Toronto Globe

Nothing except the mint can make money without advertising.
THOMAS B. MACAULAY

It is a great art to know how to sell wind.
BALTASAR GRACIAN

To sell something, tell a woman it's a bargain; tell a man it's deductible.
EARL WILSON

Everyone lives by selling something.
ROBERT LOUIS STEVENSON

Buying is cheaper than asking.
GERMAN PROVERB

People will buy anything that's one to a customer.
SINCLAIR LEWIS

Business is never so healthy as when, like a chicken, it must do a certain amount of scratching for what it gets.
HENRY FORD

To lead the people, walk behind them.
LAO-TZU

Executive ability is deciding quickly and getting someone else to do the work.
J. G. POLLARD

A man who has to be convinced to act before he acts is *not* a man of action.
GEORGES CLEMENCEAU

Young men are fitter to invent than to judge; fitter for execution than for counsel; and fitter for new projects than for settled business.
FRANCIS BACON

Leadership appears to be the act of getting others to want to do something you are convinced should be done.

VANCE PACKARD

Good management consists in showing *average* people how to do the work of *superior* people.

JOHN D. ROCKEFELLER, JR.

The secret of successful managing is to keep the five guys who hate you away from the five guys who haven't made up their minds.

CASEY STENGEL

You take all the experience and judgement of men over 50 out of the world and there wouldn't be enough left to run it.

HENRY FORD

The man who builds a factory builds a temple; the man who works there worships there; and to each is due not scorn and blame but reverence and praise.

CALVIN COOLIDGE

The question "Who ought to be boss?" is like asking "Who ought to be tenor in the quartet?" Obviously, the man who can sing tenor.

HENRY FORD

The big salaries in business always go to those who have what it takes to get things done. That is true not only of those executives who guide the destinies of a business, but it is true of those upon whom executives must depend for results.

J. C. ASPLEY

Power means not having to raise your voice.

GEORGE WILL

Power is the greatest aphrodisiac.

HENRY A. KISSINGER

A friend in power is a friend lost.

SAMUEL ADAMS

A chief is a man who assumes responsibility. He says, "I was beaten," he does not say, "My men were beaten."

ANTOINE DE SAINT-EXUPÉRY

The employer generally gets the employees he deserves.

SIR WALTER BILBEY

When you get right down to it, one of the most important tasks of a manager is to eliminate his people's excuse for failure.

ROBERT TOWNSEND

Never give up a man until he has failed at something he likes.

LEWIS E. LAWES

Big shots are only little shots who keep shooting.

CHRISTOPHER MORLEY

No man ever manages a legitimate business in this life without doing indirectly far more for other men than he is trying to do for himself.

HENRY WARD BEECHER

Committee—a group of men who keep minutes and waste hours.

MILTON BERLE

Nothing is ever accomplished by committee unless it consists of three members, one of whom happens to be sick and the other absent.

HENDRIK VAN LOON

You know, if an orange and an apple went into conference consultations, it might come out a pear.

RONALD REAGAN

Having served on various committees I have drawn up a list of rules: Never arrive on time; this stamps you as a beginner. Don't say anything until the meeting is half over; this stamps you as wise. Be as vague as possible; this avoids irritating the others. When in doubt, suggest a subcommittee be appointed. Be the first to move for adjournment; this will make you popular; it's what everyone is waiting for.

HARRY CHAPMAN

Men are never so tired and harassed as when they deal with a woman who wants a raise.

MICHAEL KORDA

Suffer women once to arrive at an equality with you, and they will from that moment become your superiors.

CATO THE CENSOR

To be successful, a woman has to be much better at her job than a man.

GOLDA MEIR

Try not to become a man of success but rather try to become a man of value.

ALBERT EINSTEIN

Always mistrust a subordinate who never finds fault with his superior.

JOHN CHURTON COLLINS

The only way to get the best of an argument is to avoid it.
DALE CARNEGIE

Good fellows are a dime a dozen, but an aggressive leader is priceless.
EARL "RED" BLAIK

Few great men could pass Personnel.
PAUL GOODMAN

A 10,000-aspirin job.
Japanese term for executive responsibility

America is the country where you buy a lifetime supply of aspirin for one dollar, and use it up in two weeks.
JOHN BARRYMORE

When you can do the common things of life in an uncommon way, you will command the attention of the world.
GEORGE WASHINGTON CARVER

Most employers these days are more interested in performance than conformance.
HENRY FORD II

Whenever you're sitting across from some important person, always picture him sitting there in a suit of long underwear. That's the way I always operated in business.

JOSEPH P. KENNEDY

The most successful highest-up executives carefully select understudies. They don't strive to do everything themselves. They train and trust others. This leaves them foot-free, mind-free, with time to think. They have time to receive important callers, to pay worthwhile visits. They have time for their families. No matter how able, any employer or executive who insists on running a one-man enterprise courts unhappy circumstances when his powers dwindle.

B. C. FORBES

The first-rate man will try to surround himself with his equals, or betters if possible. The second-rate man will surround himself with third-rate men. The third-rate man will surround himself with fifth-rate men.

ANDRÉ WEIL

They tell me I often go out on a limb. Well, that's where I like to be.

HENRY J. KAISER

When you say that you agree to a thing in principle you mean that you have not the slightest intention of carrying it out in practice.

BISMARCK

In all matters of opinion, our adversaries are insane.

MARK TWAIN

When people agree with me I always feel that I must be wrong.

OSCAR WILDE

I don't want any yes-men around me. I want everyone to tell me the truth—even though it costs him his job.

SAMUEL GOLDWYN

I have heard your views. They do not harmonize with mine. The decision is taken unanimously.

CHARLES DE GAULLE

All business sagacity reduces itself in the last analysis to a judicious use of sabotage.

THORSTEIN VEBLEN

A corporation is an artificial being, invisible, intangible, and existing only in contemplation of law.

JOHN MARSHALL

Corporation: an ingenious device for obtaining individual profit without individual responsibility.
AMBROSE BIERCE

Corporations are invisible, immortal and have no soul.
ascribed to ROGER MANWOOD, *chief baron of the English Exchequer, 1592*

Corporations are people, too.
WILLIAM SIMON

Corporations . . . are many lesser commonwealths in the bowels of a greater, like worms in the entrails of a natural man.
THOMAS HOBBES

Capitalists are no more capable of self-sacrifice than a man is capable of lifting himself by his own bootstraps.
LENIN

What is good for the country is good for General Motors, and what is good for General Motors is good for the country.
CHARLES E. WILSON

A big corporation is more or less blamed for being big; it is only big because it gives service. If it doesn't give service, it gets small faster than it grew big.
WILLIAM S. KNUDSEN

Big Business is basic to the very life of this country; and yet many—perhaps most—Americans have a deep-seated fear and an emotional repugnance to it. Here is monumental contradiction.

DAVID LILIENTHAL

Big Business is not dangerous because it is big, but because its bigness is an unwholesome inflation created by privilege and exemptions which it ought not to enjoy.

WOODROW WILSON

We demand that big business give people a square deal; in return we must insist that when anyone engaged in big business honestly endeavors to do right, he shall himself be given a square deal.

THEODORE ROOSEVELT

One cannot walk through a mass-production factory and not feel that one is in hell.

W. H. AUDEN

Going to work for a large company is like getting on a train. Are you going sixty miles an hour or is the train going sixty miles an hour and you're just sitting still.

J. PAUL GETTY

One way to avoid having industrial troubles is to avoid having industries.

DON MARQUIS

79

Retirement at sixty-five is ridiculous. When I was sixty-five I still had pimples.
GEORGE BURNS

He's no failure. He's not dead yet.
WILLIAM LLOYD GEORGE

The man who dies rich, dies disgraced.
ANDREW CARNEGIE

There is a great deal of truth in Andrew Carnegie's remark "The man who dies rich, dies disgraced." I should add, the man who lives rich, lives disgraced.
AGA KHAN III

When you have told anyone you have left him a legacy, the only decent thing to do is die at once.
SAMUEL BUTLER

There's no reason to be the richest man in the cemetery. You can't do any business from there.
COLONEL SANDERS

When I die, my epitaph should read: *She Paid the Bills.* That's the story of my private life.
GLORIA SWANSON

INDEX